HEAVEN'S PATTERN

+GOD'S DESIRE
TO MAKE A MAN

MICHAEL DOW

AUTHOR OF FASTING & THE BREAKING POINT

DEDICATION

This book is dedicated to the joyful travelers of the narrow road and its ways. For those who have tasted and seen and now cannot entrust the devotion of their heart to another. To all who have lost their lives and had their dreams swallowed up in the tenderness of His embrace. I applaud you from afar. I stand with you in heart. I rally alongside and cheer on all of you who are finding Him in rest and continually being satisfied by Him in joy. This is for you. May you continue to find Him in all of your seeking, for He is the rewarder of such faithful ones.

TABLE OF CONTENTS

Acknowledgments vii

Introduction ix

1 Desire and Design 15

2 Authorization and Invitation 25

3 Activity and Intimacy 37

4 Investment and Expectation 49

5 Followable and Reproducible 61

6 Moldable and Exportable 69

7 Luxuries and Necessities 79

8 Individuality and Legacy 93

9 Speaking and Yielding 111

Afterword 123

About the Author 127

About the Ministry 129

ACKNOWLEDGMENTS

Thank you to my wife, Anna, and children, Ariyah, Josiah, and Emma. Daily you show me Jesus and provoke me to go farther, dream bigger, and never settle. I love you with everything that I am.

Thank you to Kathy Curtis for the incredible time and work that you put in to prepare this project. Your professionalism and excellence is always a joy to work alongside. I am thankful to the Lord for connecting us.

Thank you to Blake Vasek, founder of Yobe Creative, for the great design work for this project. Your creativity and excellence have been a gift. I am honored to work alongside someone as yourself.

INTRODUCTION

As a follower of Jesus, your life is meant to give a glimpse into another world. This other world is heaven, full of awe and wonder, established upon the person of Jesus, whose likeness the Father desires to transform all of us into who believe. Since this is the Father's goal for the lives of all who come to believe, it is not enough just to simply sidestep Jesus as if He were some sort of highlight along the way towards the point that God is after. Jesus is the point that God is after. Jesus is not some highlight along the way; He *is* the way. Jesus is the point. Jesus is God's point.

We must behold Him in order to become more like Him. Beholding Jesus energizes change in your life. God is reconfiguring your life, the nature and substance of who you are, to reflect this image of His Son. God wants to get His point across in you. God is trying to make you something. However, not to be mistaken as if the something that God is working towards making you does not have a definite goal attached to it; it does. God is trying to make you like Jesus.

Your life is being built to be an invitation. This invitation is into becoming a living embodiment of heaven's value system, where your life bears the substance and culture of the Kingdom that your heart has surrendered to. Jesus, while preaching, said that the Kingdom of God was at hand.[1] We live in the tension of the Kingdom of God being now and not yet. From within that beautiful tension our lives are on display with the intention of revealing to the world around us what another world looks like.

Jesus was a man who walked among us though He was not from among us. Jesus is the man, fully God and fully human, who being from another world came and interacted with His own in their world. Jesus' life gave men the privilege of looking through the window to see what another world looked like. God, through the life of Jesus, was able to show men what the Kingdom looked like fleshed out in the life of a man walking the earth. Jesus gave us a glimpse of what it looks like for God to have a man on the ground who would fulfill the reality of the words, "Your Kingdom come, Your will be done, on earth as it is in heaven."[2]

Jesus, a man walking in this world yet surrendered to another world. A man free from the love of this world, therefore able to serve it and invite men out of

---

[1] Mark 1:15
[2] Matt. 6:10

it and into the reality of another world and the embodiment of its value system. Jesus brought the reality of another world into our world and then invited men and women into the experience and expression of it. Heaven had come because heaven's representative, Jesus the Son, had come.

Jesus brought the reality of another world into our world and then invited men and women into the experience and expression of it.

There are hungry hearts surrounding you and their desire is to see something in you that is more than just what this natural world in all of its effort and wisdom is able to produce. They long to see something more than just the perfected cycle of religious devotion devoid of the power and presence of God Himself, to whom all of their devotion is claimed to be aimed.

Hungry hearts are longing to see the revealing of a people who embody the real substance of their message. They don't just want to hear about a Kingdom; they want to see the Kingdom made manifest in the life of a man or woman in the earth. The Bible tells us that all of creation is groaning and anxiously longing for the revealing of the sons of God.[3] The revealing

---

[3] Rom. 8:19

of a people who won't simply forfeit substance with a "Do as I say and not as I do" type approach to life with Jesus.

There are those who have become well acquainted with how to do godly works. There are those who have perfected the frequenting of godly activities and gatherings. There are many who spend countless hours trying to protect the imagery that they have constructed, built upon perception. Then there are those who bear in their life the substance of God that has brought real transformation to the makeup of who they are as individuals.

Their real life has been reconfigured. They have been changed. They are no longer the same thing that they used to be. Their life is not one constructed with smoke and mirrors, the reality of which is hidden behind the perfect screening of activity and responsibility, which at times becomes the best shield for issues beneath the surface. The burning desire of our hearts should be for God to make us something that we could never simply manufacture or fake. Change us, Lord!

There is a great difference between someone who says, "I know how to behave this way if the circumstances are set up in my favor," and then the man who says, "I actually am this, regardless of what position or assignment in life I am experiencing." One has the potential to live something if all of life's scenarios are set up a certain way, yet knows in his heart he has not yet become this reality that God has for us. The other has experienced real transformation in his walk with the Lord to where he has actually been made something different, something new.

The talk is no longer about what a man simply knows how to do, but what that man has actually become. The discussion goes from satisfactory activity to living embodiment. That man that has become is no longer trying to fake it till he makes it because that man has been made.

God's desire is to make men. The gift of God in salvation is something that you can receive for free. However, being made by God will cost you everything. There is no easy road to spiritual maturity in God. There are no yellow-brick-road shortcuts into gaining real substance in your spiritual life. There is no fast-forward button.

There is one road that has been laid out in front of all men leading to this desired outcome. The path is narrow. The crowd on the beginning stages of this journey are full. However, as you continue down this path you start to realize that the crowd thins. People fade. Satisfaction with gimmicks and illusions are embraced. This is not God's way. God is not interested in gimmicks, and He is surely not a magician.

God desires a people. The people God desires are ordinary people filled with an extraordinary God. In fact, God is building this people that He desires right now by the work and processing of the Holy Spirit. These people are an embodiment of another world and its value system being lived out in a day-to-day practical reality that powerfully transcends and transforms the bondages that cripple men to a current environment and systematic way of natural, or fleshly, thinking and living. These people that God is building have chosen, by transformation, to live a higher way. There is a higher way. Jesus lived above, though He walked below.

The question is not can God do it...of course He can. He can do it. He has done it. He did it in Jesus. He has done it in countless others. If God can do it in one man, He can do it in any man. The real question is this...can God do it in you? I pray so.

Let us begin our journey...

CHAPTER 01

DESIRE AND DESIGN

For through Him we both have our access in one Spirit to the Father. So, then you are no longer strangers and aliens, but you are fellow citizens with the saints, of God's household, having been built on the foundation of the apostles and prophets, Christ Jesus Himself being the cornerstone...[4]

God goes to great lengths to make men. This has always been God's way. Of all the many things that

---

[4] Eph. 2:18-20

God has in His arsenal, His chosen means by which He is transforming the world is through the lives of real people. God is using the lives of real people to change the world. This has been the case in every generation. If this were not the chosen method, Jesus would not have come as a man. Jesus coming as a man reveals, and further confirms, God's commitment to using men to transform the world. We cannot lose sight of this. God is building everything off of people, because God is building everything off of Jesus.

It is God's desire to build everything off of Jesus. God did not just send Jesus into the world for the sake of introduction. God's introduction of Jesus was with the wholehearted intention for the reproduction of Jesus. God wanted to introduce Jesus so that He could begin to reproduce Jesus. Jesus is the firstborn among many sons and daughters.[5] We will talk about this a little more in depth later. But let it suffice for now, and the point that we are developing here, to say that God is building everything off of His cornerstone, Jesus the Son. Jesus is what God is saying and doing.

What do I mean by this? I mean that everything that God is doing, saying, and building is being established upon the person of Jesus. God is unwilling to bypass Jesus to build anything. We can look into the

---

[5] Rom. 8:29

words of Paul penned to the church at Ephesus to gain some clarity.

Paul, in writing to the Ephesian believers, says to them that they are now fellow citizens of God's household, and that this household has been built on the foundation of apostles and prophets, Christ Jesus Himself being the cornerstone.[6] By definition a cornerstone is something that is essential or indispensable. Another definition for a cornerstone is the chief foundation on which something is constructed or developed.

Jesus, according to our verse that we just read, is the cornerstone, so therefore we can conclude that Jesus is essential and indispensable. We can also determine that Jesus is the foundation for all construction and development. Jesus is the foundation for all of God's building, the means by which God is building, and the outcome to which God is building.

This seems too simple and elementary when stated this way, but let's take a moment to consider the implications of such a statement. Jesus is what God is using to build? We must find great encouragement in these words because Jesus was a real person. Jesus was not just some ministry strategy conjured up in the mind of God. Jesus wasn't some relevant scheme that would

---

[6] Eph. 2:19-20

bend and fade according to the cultural rhythms of the day that He entered into. Jesus wasn't a man who had a lot of charisma and ranked high in His "likability," therefore God thought it was a great plan. It wasn't because Jesus "fit the demographic" of the people that God was trying to reach. You get the point here; there is no need to continue belaboring the examples.

Jesus is the cornerstone because of who He is, and not simply because of what He can do. It is the actual makeup, the substance, of who He is that makes Him worthy to be built upon. The character of Jesus, the actual makeup, the real substance, is what God is using to build. This cannot be overlooked. The success and strength of all that is being built in our day for God will be held up against God's standard, His pattern, which is the character of His Son, Jesus.

No matter how flashy. No matter how seemingly successful. No matter the applause that is generated, or the accolades that are acquired. No matter the money raised, or the crowds gathered. No matter the hype created, or the influence attained. If in the end it does not pass the sifting of the character of Jesus, it has all been in vain. God is interested in forming the image of His Son into men and He will not bypass this desire in order to appease the desires of people.

God is forming and fashioning men into the image of His Son; it is His goal.[7] God is transforming the lives of real people into the image of Jesus. Following Jesus is a matter of transformation. God is transforming people who then transform people, homes, cities, regions, and nations. The transformed ones get sent to be an agent of transformation. The transformed ones become sent ones, sent into every sphere of life and influence to be agents of radical and powerful transformation.

> **God is forming and fashioning men into the image of His Son; it is His goal.**

Jesus was a "sent one," sent from the heavens into the earth to live among men with the declaration and demonstration of another Kingdom. However, Jesus' life was not just sent for declaration and demonstration, but also for the sake of invitation. Jesus invited men into what He actually carried in and upon His own life. Jesus carried the culture of the Kingdom in and upon His life, His real life. Jesus' life is what God looked to build off of.

God wants to change your life so that He can build off of your life. Your real life, not just the gifts that you carry. Your real life, and not just some learned abilities.

---

[7] Rom. 8:29

Both gifts and learned abilities can be great shields to keep people from ever being able to see who and what you actually are. John Maxwell says it this way, "You teach all that you know, but you actually reproduce who and what you really are."[8] It is God's desire and design to build upon the life of a real person. A real person formed in reality, and into God's reality.

We find God's desire to build, or multiply, the life of a real person in His encounter that He has with Abram in Genesis chapter 17. The Bible says, "When Abram was ninety-nine years old, the Lord appeared to Abram and said to him, "I am God Almighty; Walk before Me and be blameless. I will establish My covenant between Me and you, and I will multiply you exceedingly.""[9] God's desire was to multiply the life of Abram. Not some gift that Abram carried. Not just some task that Abram knew how to do, regardless of the excellence that it could be offered with. What God had in mind would come out of the life of who Abram really was.

One chapter later we find God again in the place of encounter with Abram, who is now Abraham because of God renaming him, speaking of how He is going to fulfill this great call that He has put on Abraham's

---

[8] John Maxwell, *How to Influence People*, (Nashville: Thomas Nelson, 2013), 62.

[9] Gen. 17:1-2

life to be a father of many nations. Listen closely to what God says, "Since Abraham will surely become a great and mighty nation, and in him all the nations of the earth will be blessed. For I have chosen him, so that he may command his children and his household after him to keep the way of the Lord by doing righteousness and justice, so that the Lord may bring upon Abraham what He has spoken to him."[10]

Everything that God is desiring to do through the life of Abraham will begin by Abraham going home first. The way that God is going to multiply him exceedingly and bless all the nations of the earth is by sending Abraham home first to lead his children and his household well. When was the last time that someone encouraged you this way? The way that God is going to do everything that He has spoken to you is to first send you home?

Who you are at home is who you are. Home represents transparency. Home represents reality. The who you are at home is representative of who God knows you to be when no one else is watching, the real you. If you can get it right at home, you can get it right anywhere. If you can touch those who are in your own house, you can touch the world. God needs you to win at home with those closest to you, who know

---

[10] Gen. 18:18-19

you best, before you attempt to go running around the world trying to win. Abraham was a sent one, but he was first sent home to lead well and be a man of real substance.

Please do not read these words and miss the entire point because of the mention of "sent ones." These words do not create an immediate exemption for you. These words to do not give you a way out of somehow being held accountable. You have definitely been sent. You have been sent into a specific sphere of influence to represent Jesus.

It may be to some children that you are chasing around every day, but God is looking for you to be an agent of transformation. It may be at the business that you lead. It may be at a cubicle at a big-time corporation. It may be at a corner store. It may be on your school campus. The *where you are* is not as important as the *who you are*. Once you allow God to bring real change to the who, the where can be anywhere!

The *where you are* is not as important as the *who you are*. Once you allow God to bring real change to the who, the where can be anywhere!

This is the point we are getting to. Jesus wasn't only Jesus in the heavens. He wasn't only true to who God knew Him to be in some faraway abstract place that didn't have any real bearing in our experience of life as we know it. Jesus was introduced here by God and walked among us in authenticity and power. Jesus did not violate or compromise the who He was regardless of where He was. And now, because of His faithful life lived before God in the power of the Spirit, God the Father is able to begin His process of reproduction with the life of His Son who has become the pattern, or the cornerstone.

This is what the introduction of Jesus was for. Jesus was introduced so that He could then be reproduced in countless people that would come to believe.

God wants to reproduce the life of Jesus in you and cause you to become an agent of transformation to any and all around you. This is what the introduction of Jesus was for. Jesus was introduced so that He could then be reproduced in countless people that would come to believe. God unveiled His Son and is now unveiling the life of His Son in those who lay their lives down to Him. God is putting together a bride for His Son with the lives of such beautiful ones. The extraordinary God inside of ordinary people changing the world in extraordinary ways.

AUTHORIZATION AND INVITATION

Authorization:
- The act of authorizing
- Permission or power granted by an authority

In the last chapter, we established the point that God introduced Jesus so that He could reproduce Jesus. I believe that Jesus was very aware of what God was doing all along. I don't think that Jesus was left out in the dark or that He was totally oblivious to the plan of God to sow His life into the earth in order to multiply His life in people. Jesus knew. Of course, He knew.

He still knows. That's why His invitation to men was, is, and will always be, into His life, and to His life. The invitation is unchanging.

At the conclusion of Jesus' talk with the people on the side of the mount in Matthew's gospel we are given two verses that are very intriguing. The verses are found at the very end of chapter 7, verses 28 and 29. They are intriguing because they provide profound insight into our conversation that is developing. These verses bring a close to a section in the Bible that has become known as the Sermon on the Mount. Others use the description, the Constitution of the Kingdom. Whatever your description for these chapters may be, we will pick it up at the last two verses of Matthew chapter 7.

"When Jesus had finished saying these things, the crowds were amazed at His teaching, because He taught as one who had authority, and not as the teachers of the law."[11] The way that these verses are written create a unique tension that we must deal with. Matthew says that when Jesus spoke it was taken very differently by those that were listening. There was a different response to the hearers when Jesus spoke. The crowd had a different sense after hearing the

---

[11] Matt. 7:28-29

words of Jesus. And why? Because they recognized that He taught as one who had real authority.

There was something different when Jesus spoke. The difference in Jesus' speaking brought immediate confrontation to the claimed authority of the teachers of the law. Jesus was not calling them out, at least not here; He was simply teaching.

Jesus was not directly confrontational to the teachers of the law in His approach on this day. He just taught the people that gathered around Him. It was the real authority that Jesus carried that exposed the lack of authority of others who were teaching. On this day Jesus did not have to speak directly against what was not real. He simply spoke to and out of what was real, and all that wasn't real and genuine from God became glaringly obvious to those who were gathered listening.

> **It was the real authority that Jesus carried that exposed the lack of authority of others who were teaching.**

Why would this happen? Jesus wasn't just teaching about things that He had learned. He wasn't sitting on the side of the mount trying to wow people with spiritual information in order to gain influence. He wasn't manipulating a public-speaking gift in order to become an authority on a specific topic. He sat down and opened up His heart. He spoke directly out of

His own life. This issue at hand is that Jesus is the embodiment of the information that he was communicating. This created a very real difference, an issue with a matter of authority at stake.

Jesus embodied the talk He was having. He wasn't speaking out of a simple head knowledge of the right information. Jesus, in and of Himself, was the right information. He was speaking out of His life, what He actually was. Jesus embodied the substance of the talk. We have to understand that Matthew chapters 5 through 7 are not simply just a list of spiritual information used for the sake of behavioral modification.

The bridge to cross the seemingly unattainable gap of this other-worldly incredible life that Jesus was speaking about was, is, and will always be, the life of Jesus.

Jesus didn't just sit down, speak powerful words to all of the people, and then wave goodbye. He didn't create the tension and then not provide a solution. He provided the solution. Jesus pointed at Himself for the solution. He is the solution. The bridge to cross the seemingly unattainable gap of this other-worldly incredible life that Jesus was speaking about was, is, and will always be, the life of Jesus. He was inviting people to and into His life.

Jesus sat on the side of the mount that day and painted a beautiful vision of what life could be like. He powerfully articulated what God was doing and

> **The way that Jesus directed people's attention to what God was doing was to point to Himself.**

how He was doing it. However, at the end of the talk Jesus did something a little different than what most were ready for.

Jesus didn't communicate a powerful vision and then step out of the way. He didn't say, "Look at this, but don't look at Me." In fact, Jesus did the exact opposite. He communicated a powerful vision of what God was doing, and then to their surprise I am sure, He stepped in the way. Jesus stepped in the way and said, "If all of that sounds great, look at Me, because I am what God is doing!"

This needs to be said again. Jesus put Himself directly in the way of what He knew about what God was doing. As troubling as this was for many, it didn't matter to Him, because He knew that it was true. The way that Jesus directed people's attention to what God was doing was to point to Himself. This cannot be overstated enough. Jesus wasn't hiding behind a great vision that God gave Him; *He was* God's great vision.

It is too easy in our day to hide a bankrupt individual behind a breathtaking vision. It happens all the time. People say, "Look at this, but don't look at me. Look at the good that we will do. Look at the lives that are being changed. Look at the applause that is being generated. However, please keep all of your attention on this, the vision, and do not for one moment attempt to move your eyes from *what* we are doing to focus in on *who* is actually doing it."

There is a separation many times that is heartbreaking. The people of Jesus' day understood this tragedy all too well. The Pharisees **God's building** and other religious elect would **program looks** communicate a standard, or a way **like Jesus.** of life, that they themselves were not even living. However, they were benefiting off the appearance being kept intact, and this was more than enough for them.

This was not enough for Jesus. Being very aware of the tension that He would be perceived as others that were casting vision in His day, He articulated, and then directed all attention to Himself. This, I am sure, shattered the expectations of the people listening.

God's building program looks like Jesus. Jesus understood very well that He was what God was doing. This is why He felt the need to unveil Himself. He understood very well that He was the very thing that God was doing; He was what God was seeking to reproduce. The Sermon on the Mount is the great unveiling of the Son.

Jesus pulled the curtain back and gave people a glimpse. He opened up the window to His life and showed people what He was made of, the real makeup, the characteristics that He actually embodied. He wasn't just attempting to transfer information; He was inviting people into real transformation. The matters of the Kingdom have never simply been about the transfer of the right information, but rather, it has always, and will always be, a matter of transformation. The authority on Jesus' life allowed God to issue invitations through His life.

Following Jesus is a matter of transformation. This is something that sounds so elementary, yet is missing in so many. Coming to Jesus, being empowered by the Holy Spirit to lay your life down, and following after Him is not a matter of spending the rest of your life simply being informed. Some believe that coming to Jesus is just about receiving new information on how to do life. This could not be farther from the truth. This is a great insult to the incredible extent that God has gone in order to set you up to succeed.

Jesus has opened up a way to make you something new, and is literally "making you" something new as you follow Him.

You have not been granted an opportunity to succeed because you now simply just have new information to govern an old life. You have been set up to succeed because you have been given the opportunity to be transformed. Jesus has opened up a way to make you something new, and is literally "making you" something new as you follow Him.

The something that He is making you is not something that you can fake it until you make it. The something that you are being made into is something that you can't make yourself any other way. Your life of following Jesus is not about how well you can imitate Jesus' behaviors, but rather, how well you can yield to God's work in you to make your life the real quality and embodiment of, not only Jesus' behaviors, but the character and substance that motivates and animates those behaviors.

It is the Holy Spirit working in and with you to perfect the work that God began in you. It is the Holy Spirit working in you by way of relentlessly revealing Jesus to you that is constantly empowering your invitation to be made more like Jesus. God is opening your eyes to the beauty and reality of who Jesus is and what He is like, and then fervently working in you to reconfigure the substance of your life to become what He has shown you in Christ. This process goes beyond just receiving the right information on how to do life.

The world is flooded with people that have acquired the right information, and yet, though they have obtained the right information, that information is not producing in their lives and bringing them to the right outcomes. This is a great tragedy. We live in a day where men can communicate the right information without embodying the substance of what they are communicating.

People use the right information for the sake of being impressive, being appreciated, gaining an advantage in any given moment, or a million other reasons that would present themselves. People hide behind information. It happens every day. People communicate things with their lips that their actual life doesn't bear the substance of. This should not be. Our lives were not meant to be well put together exteriors, held together by a plethora of the right information, and yet, shallow unchanged interiors.

There must come a point in your life when all of what you have heard, by way of information, gets touched by the Spirit and becomes revelation to you. Information alone doesn't empower invitation to transformation, but revelation does. Revelation allows invitation to transformation to become real in your life. The Holy Spirit bringing illumination to certain information that you have heard or stored up over years, can in a moment, cause that dry information to be powerfully charged with invitation when it becomes revelation to you.

With these truths in mind, this is what brings us back to Jesus, the pattern Son. Jesus embodied the fullness of the words He spoke. Jesus didn't just offer information to people; Jesus offered invitations to people. You cannot invite people into what you yourself have not been given access to. Jesus was able to make invitations because His life bore the substance of the invitation.

The substance of your life is what authorizes invitations to come through your life.

The substance of your life is what authorizes invitations to come through your life. You may be able to give descriptions and definitions with the right information, but you will never issue invitations. When you embody the substance of a specific reality, God can then issue invitations to men through your life. Your life becomes the invitation. The reality of what God has made you becomes the invitation.

Jesus knew that He was an invitation. He said it clearly Himself, "Come to Me, all who are weary..."[12] I can hear it in the heart of Jesus... "Come to Me, yield to Me, and let Me live in you! Abide in Me and

---

[12] Matt. 11:28

let Me be Myself in you. Stop wearying yourself with all of your "trying" to be more like Me. Spend the rest of your life enjoying Me as I enjoy you, and in the place of pure enjoyment, let Me reveal Myself in and through your life to a degree that you could have never worked up in all of your own efforts and strength. Let Me transform you so that I can reproduce you. Let Me make you so that I can multiply you!"

Will you allow God to put you in the middle of what He is doing? The point is not just for amazing things to happen *through* you, or even *all around* you, without them first and most importantly happening *in* you. The authenticity of what God has done, and is doing in you, is what grants you the authority.

Simply put, authority is found in authenticity. Authenticity doesn't come as a byproduct of articulation. Just because you know how to communicate something does not always mean that the power of the something that you know how to talk has really been wrought into the fabric of the reality of your life by the Spirit. We must contend for this. It is too important to go on without. Do not allow your life to fall into the category of those who were familiar in Jesus' day, that just found a way to benefit and make a living off of their lack of authenticity. God has a better way!

ACTIVITY AND INTIMACY

"Many will say to Me on that day, 'Lord, Lord, did we not prophesy in Your name and in Your name, drive out demons, and in Your name, perform many miracles?' Then I will tell them plainly, 'I never knew you. Away from Me, you evildoers!' "[13]

God makes men through intimacy with Himself. There is no way around this. Time with God is

---

[13] Matt. 7:22-23

unavoidable for the man that seeks to be made by God. Time, alone, behind closed doors. This is the painful truth for those who seek quick fixes. This is the buyout clause for many who enroll hoping that God will surprise them one day with new information on a cheaper solution to the same destination. Though men wait for something new, God remains the same. His way is proven. His process is tested and found faithful. God brings men to and into Himself.

If God is not enough, no other temporary solution will matter, or make a difference.

If God is not enough, no other temporary solution will matter, or make a difference. Though it may seem to hold up or produce for a time being, in the end it will prove false. Methods and mechanics that don't have their rooting and bearings in the person of God will eventually crumble to circumstantial tensions. God alone stands victorious over men's formulas attempting to become by themselves through lesser means than what God has prescribed.

The simple and scary truth is this: Men can act like God independent of God Himself. But, in the midst of this crisis, we must be reminded of this beautiful truth: God wants activity that has its origin in intimacy. Men become easily satisfied with being busy, yet

God is not satisfied until they have been built. God's great desire is not to simply busy men, but to make them. God is after the making of a man. God is trying to actually make you something and not just get you to do something. We must not only hear this truth, but believe it and apply it to the deepest parts of our hearts and lives, especially in the place of our motives.

We live in a day where men are impressed with what others seem to be doing. There is a supreme value put upon activities. The entry point into the conversation of appreciation comes with a high buy-in of results. Results dominate conversations. People are constantly pressured into feeling like they need to have a better story, a better testimony, a better "thing" happening than others do in order to feel like they have a place.

We must be careful that we don't get caught up in the whirlwind of pressure that drags people into activities in order to feel like they belong. The risk is that the pressure to preform becomes so great that it begins to supersede all other things. Performance for the sake of approval. Performance for the sake of attention and appreciation. Performance in order to feel as if my life is being counted in the larger story that God is writing. Performance becomes the

God is trying to actually make you something and not just get you to do something.

validator in order for whatever chair I am sitting in to have its right to belong at the table.

With all of the tension to perform we must be cautious. We must be cautious that we don't find ourselves outperforming everyone around us, and yet ending up in the crowd that is found in Matthew chapter 7. What crowd, you ask? Great question, I am glad you asked. Let's take a few moments to look into exactly what kind of crowd is found in the seventh chapter of Matthew's gospel.

In Matthew chapter 7 Jesus is talking to a crowd of people that have gathered on that day. His references point to many things, including judging others, prayer, and the narrow and wide gates. Then towards the end of chapter 7 He begins a portion of the discussion that covers a tree and its fruit. He moves from there and discusses false prophets.[14] Then He speaks about a specific crowd of people that He would be face-to-face with on that day. That day being the day that all men will stand before Him and give an account of their lives. This is where we find our point.

Jesus says, "Many will say to Me on that day, 'Lord, Lord, did we not prophesy in Your name, and in Your name cast out demons, and in Your name, perform many miracles?' And then I will declare to them, 'I

---

[14] Matt. 7:1-20

never knew you; depart from Me, you who practice lawlessness."[15] This seems like a pretty intense situation given its context. This is the great day that all will stand before Jesus and give an account for the deeds done in the flesh while living.[16] This is definitely the day that I would not want to have to hear these words come out of the mouth of Jesus, at least not in reference to my life, that's for sure.

As intense as this would seem, let's take a minute and actually break down what is happening here to see if we can make things simpler and plain. This is without a doubt a moment where the most important conversation that any of us have had is going to take place. I know that you probably think that you've had some important conversations over the course of your life but I guarantee you that none are going to top this one. The most important conversation that we will ever have is going to be on the day that we stand before Jesus. This talk with Jesus will be the most important talk.

In terms of the crowd that He was speaking to that day, we need to understand that Jesus said *many*. He didn't say a few. He didn't say a handful of select individuals. *Many* was His choice for word selection. Many is important. Many means that we cannot afford

---

[15] Matt. 7:22-23
[16] 2 Cor. 5:10

to miss the implications of His word choice. Jesus is the author and the finisher. Jesus is the beginning and the end. He knows what He is saying, what it means, and how it will be taken; and yet He says it anyway. We must not miss this.

The many that are standing before Jesus on that day have a response in the conversation that is happening. Jesus tells us what their response is, "Lord, Lord, but did we not do these things…didn't we prophesy, drive out demons, and in Your name, perform many miracles?"[17] There is something about this that I just can't seem to understand. There is something about their response that is extremely puzzling to me. In fact, I am appalled that this would be the case considering the moment that is unfolding.

In the moment where it would appear that everything is riding on the line. In a moment of time where everything is hanging in the balance. This is the moment where the many, individually, have an opportunity to speak to Jesus and validate the entirety of their lives. This is the moment where either you are going to get in, or be left out forever. You would think that in this moment what is said would be well thought out and very intentional on the part of the many.

---

[17] Matt. 7:22

In this moment before Jesus, the many on that day, by saying, "But did we not do these things...," choose to point to the activity that filled their life as a way to bring validation to the entirety of their life. In the moment, as we've already established, where it would seem to matter the most, they choose to point to prophesy, power, and performance. The best that the many could come up with as a solution to the current dilemma was to point to what they were doing, the activity of their life as a way to get Jesus to accept their life.

This doesn't seem to add up to me. Why didn't it go a little differently? Why couldn't it have gone something like this: "Jesus, because I loved You. Because I knew You. Because I walked with You. Because I knew Your presence and Your voice, and was overwhelmed by Your embrace. I gave my life to You. I was frequently with You behind the door, in my closet. I gave the entirety of my life over to You in the developing of intimacy with You."

Why didn't they point to intimacy when it seemed to matter most? Why didn't they look at Jesus face-to-face, eye to eye, and point to the intimacy that governed and animated their lives? Over the years that I've walked with Jesus, one thing that I know to be true is this: Activity will never take the place of intimacy. Activity will never be an effective substitute for intimacy. Generating a lot of activity in your life will never be a way to secure intimacy in your life.

This doesn't seem to be right. This can't be. The many on that day said that they were prophesying, casting out demons, and raising the dead. This is a group of folks that seem to be doing more than most. How many do you know that are prophesying, casting out demons, and raising the dead? Are you doing these things?

This is a group of people that seemed to have it going on. This would be a crowd of folks that you and I would've looked at from the outside, all that was visible from the activity of their life on the outside of their life, and we would've thought to ourselves, *Wow they are anointed. God must really be with them.* Yet, how is it that they ended up in a crowd of people that Jesus said He didn't know?

You need to understand something here. The gifting on your life is not a guaranteed ticket into heaven. This may make you a little uneasy, but it is true. The purpose of the gifting on your life is to reveal Jesus through your life. Let's be a little more honest, being gifted isn't even a guarantee that you are walking with Jesus Himself. You can be incredibly gifted, flow in gifts, prophesy, read people's mail, and not even walk with the Lord or have an intimate relationship with him. The activity of your life is not always an expression of the intimacy in your life with Jesus. At times, this can be far from the reality of what it actually all looks like beneath the surface, at a heart level.

Being gifted doesn't bring any guarantees into your life. Being gifted doesn't mean that you are a great spouse, a great parent, a great friend, or even someone that is great to be around. The gifting doesn't create guarantees. In fact, you can be super gifted, and yet, be a total jerk. You can be super gifted, and yet, your marriage may be falling apart and you may have a completely nonexistent relationship with your kids. You can be incredibly gifted and have a lot of hidden items in your closet.

The activity of your life is not always an expression of the intimacy in your life with Jesus.

The point is this: A great gift doesn't make you a great person. It would help if you understood something here. Jesus isn't impressed with how gifted you are. He isn't wowed by how gifted you are. He doesn't get overwhelmed watching you work with all of what He gave to you in the first place. In reality, to be brutally honest, again, you can work a gift and not walk with God.

People will always point to activity when they lack intimacy. Out of the abundance of the heart the mouth will speak.[18] In other words, what is in your heart will always eventually come out of your mouth. And for those whose hearts are dominated by activity, it will be the highlight of their speech, and in fact, how they validate their lives. And by validating their own lives this way, they will create standards by which they validate the lives of others around them. Though it may seem to impress the crowds, it will never be enough, by itself, to satisfy Jesus.

There is no amount of activity that will ever take the place of intimacy. We must guard our hearts lest we fall more in love with the work of the Lord instead of the Lord of the work. We must be very aware of the temptation to receive something from the Lord that would capture the affection of our hearts in a greater way than Jesus Himself. At the end of the day the only thing that truly satisfies the heart of a man is the presence of the One who created the heart.

We must guard our hearts lest we fall more in love with the work of the Lord instead of the Lord of the work.

Jesus is the ultimate satisfier. We must find a real place of satisfaction in Jesus outside of anything that He has given us or asked us to do. The only man who

---

[18] Luke 6:45

truly knows if he is satisfied with Jesus himself is the man who has been left all alone with nothing but Jesus Himself.

In the midst of all the crowding temptation for men to fall lustfully after the business and activities of life, God waits. God waits for a man that He can draw to Himself. God is not intimidated by your working, but He wants your working to flow from a place of loving Jesus and being intimately connected to Him on a daily basis. All of your doing must flow out of your loving, and not vice versa.

At the end of the day the only thing that truly satisfies the heart of a man is the presence of the One who created the heart.

At times, God is successful in His desire to make a man. At times, God wins in the heart and life of a man and is able to do with the life of that man all things because that man has found all things in the satisfaction of God. Has God won in your heart? God desires that you become such a one!

CHAPTER 04

INVESTMENT AND EXPECTATION

John answered and said, "A man can receive nothing, except it be given him from heaven."[19]

God is looking for a man that He can make and synchronize with Himself. Jesus, our pattern, the greatest example of what humanity should look like when filled with God, gave us great insight into the heart of the Father when He spoke these words, "Truly, truly, I say to you, the Son can do nothing of

---

[19] John 3:27

Himself, unless it is something He sees the Father doing; for whatever the Father does, these things the Son does in like manner.[20]

God desires a man, made one with Him in the place of sweet experience and exchange. God desires a man so united to Him, that that man would be unwilling to do anything outside of what would keep his life in rhythm with God.

What is God's great investment? Simply put…it is Himself. God has invested Himself into you.

Later in His life, we find Jesus again speaking, and saying these words, "For I have come down from heaven, not to do My own will, but the will of Him who sent Me."[21] Now, you are probably thinking to yourself, "Who wouldn't want that? Why would anybody not fight to keep their life in this place that is being described?"

To one who has genuinely seen the Lord and been impacted by Him in a deep way, the only reasonable response is to empty your life into loving obedience. Obeying Jesus is an expression of love. Our lives, united to Him, the surrendering of our wills to God in deep, intimate fellowship, should produce obedience. Our doing should flow continually from the place of

[20] John 5:19
[21] John 6:38

our loving, and not the opposite. Our doing should never be in hopes that it will generate loving.

I understand that this may sound like a no-brainer to you. This is the goal of all of our lives: being united to, and synchronized with God in a place of deep intimacy and power. After all, God has gone to incredible lengths in order to empower this possibility. What do I mean? I mean, God has a great investment in your life. It's true. In fact, it's very true. What is God's great investment? Simply put…it is Himself. God has invested Himself into you.

Greater than all of the talent you may have, is God Himself. Greater than all of the gifting or abilities that you have learned along the way, is God Himself. God is the greatest investment that you have received. God gave His life for you **God gave His life for you so that He could get His life into you.** so that He could get His life into you. God's ultimate goal was never simply to have the life of God remain on the outside of men, but rather, for the life of God to finally be able to get on the inside of men.

God has always wanted to get Himself into you. Your life before God was never intended to be lived without life from God. God has supplied the means by which you can be united to Him and continually remain in sync with Him…and that is the life that He Himself provides to those who abide in Him.

If we will abide in Him we have a higher probability of remaining in sync with Him. Synchronization with God is not a guarantee. Much of the success of our synchronization is dependent upon the will of the individual walking with God. The sad truth is that many find themselves doing things regularly that are not being fueled by the life of God in the place of obedience. How can this be? Jesus said, "I am the vine, you are the branches; he who abides in Me and I in him, he bears much fruit, for apart from Me you can do nothing."[22]

Let's get something clear before we continue. Jesus is not expecting that you do nothing. In fact, this is a falsification. Don't think that for one minute God would go to such great lengths in order to get His life into you in order to have you sit around and do absolutely nothing with it. This would be a tremendous waste. God has high expectations for the investment that He has made into your life.

God expects you to change the world. You may think that is not possible from where you are sitting. You may survey the current landscape of your life and be discouraged when you consider what the pieces

---

[22] John 15:5

are that you have to work with. Even in spite of this, however you may appraise your immediate surroundings, you cannot avoid being accountable to this truth: God expects for you to change the world.

You may not be called to bring radical transformation to all the nations of the world, but you are definitely called to bring transformation to your world. It may not consist of boarding planes and visiting peoples of other tribes and tongues, but you are definitely expected to do something with what God has deposited into your life. You may not be asked to change the entire world, but you are called to change your world, and that's a fact! Let's return to the words of Jesus.

You may not be asked to change the entire world, but you are called to change your world, and that's a fact!

"You can do nothing without me..."[23] This is a strange way to put it. It would make more sense to hear something like, "You can't do anything without Me." Or, "Without Me, you can't do anything." We would be more familiar with statements such as these other options. However, that is not what Jesus had to say. Jesus said that we can do *nothing* without Him.

---

[23] John 15:5

Here is the truth that Jesus is driving into our hearing and our hearts by issuing such a statement: We can get a lot of nothing done without Him. A lot of nothing. A lot of activity that doesn't have any eternal significance. There can be a tremendous amount of activity done in the name of the Lord that doesn't actually have the involvement of the Lord Himself.

This is what Jesus is speaking to. Jesus is speaking to "stuff" that is accomplished with the mask of results. But, you see, in Jesus' eyes, results are not the same as fruit. They can be the same thing, at times. However, results and fruit, at times, can be very different.

In John chapter 3 we find a situation where John the Baptist is confronted by his disciples. John's disciples are noticing a problem that is developing. There is a new guy up the block, His name is Jesus, and He is gaining influence with the people. In fact, Jesus is gaining so much influence, to the point where even some that were a part of John's crowd are leaving and going to follow after this new guy in town. John's disciples don't really like the way things are panning out and so they bring their concern to John.

They came to John and said to him, "Rabbi, that man who was with you on the other side of the Jordan—the one you testified about—look, He is baptizing, and everyone is going to Him." To this John replied, "A person can receive only what is given them from heaven…"[24] Why would John respond like this? Didn't John care that his ministry responsibility was shrinking? That doesn't seem to be right, I mean, to give your life in obedience only to have your results diminish. John understood a beautiful truth that we must grasp, and we find it bright and shining in the way that he chooses to respond to his disciples.

John says, "A man can receive only what is given him from heaven…"[25] Please take note of what he did not say. He did not say, "A man can't make anything happen." "A man is not able to produce big-time results." "A man is not able to manipulate his social network in order to advance." "A man will never be able to gain access to certain opportunities and realms of influence." John didn't say any of these; he simply stated that a man cannot receive anything from heaven unless it is given to him.

What is John really saying? John is really saying this: Fruit does not have an earthly source; its source is heavenly. Results on the other hand? Results do not always have a heavenly source. Results and fruit can have the same source, and can even indeed be intertwined. The sad reality is that sometimes we cannot tell the difference. Again, we live in a time where people put a high level of appreciation on results. Results are

---

[24] John 3:26-27
[25] John 3:27

a major motivator for some in the way that they define success in their life. At whatever the cost, results must be had. This doesn't seem to be John's approach. John found his success in obeying the voice of God.

John recognized that it would not have been worth fighting for something that God was not fighting for also. Was John really going to play the game, and fight for significance, and attempt to gain people back from following Jesus? Seriously? For what? In order to keep the perspective of importance alive in the eyes of his disciples? So that people wouldn't talk about how his crowds were shrinking? So that he could keep his voice at the table, in the conversation, when people start asking around, "So, how many did you have this past week?"

John didn't care anything for it. John was totally outside of such a thought process because he had already recognized and committed his life to what mattered most. John had found the presence and voice of the bridegroom and that is what he wasn't willing to live without.

The bride belongs to the bridegroom. The friend who attends the bridegroom waits and listens for him, and is full of joy when he hears the bridegroom's voice. That joy is mine, and it is now complete. He must become greater; I must become less.[26] John had been synchronized with God.

Remember, it was John that spent the majority of his life in the wilderness with God. It was from this place that John had an appearing.[27] John understood what a fruitful life looked like for him. John saw through the results-chasing game. Do you? John understood that if he would've acquired people back he would've impressed people, but not God. There may have been a thunderous applause from the crowds around John, but what is that worth if it goes without a simultaneous thunderous applause from heaven?

From the outside, it is hard to tell who falls into what lane, and when they do. All we get to see is people moving. And most of us give people the benefit of the doubt and believe that they are obeying the Lord. But, the only person who really knows if they are obeying the Lord or not is the person who is actually moving. We get to see action, because it is an external thing. We do not get to see motive, for it is an internal thing. Motive is a matter of the heart. Motive doesn't tell us "what"; it tells us "why" and "how."

I know you think that everybody has pure motive. Oh, how I wish that this were true. This is not something new that is only being confronted in the days

---

[26] John 3:29-30
[27] Mark 1:4

of our generation. This is actually an age-old issue. Paul spoke of these things when he penned, "It's true that some are preaching out of jealousy and rivalry. But others preach Christ with pure motives." He goes on to say, "Those others do not have pure motives as they preach about Christ. They preach with selfish ambition, not sincerely, intending to make my chains more painful to me. But that doesn't matter. Whether motives are false or genuine, the message about Christ is being preached either way, so I rejoice."[28]

Results are not the same as fruit. Results can be manipulated; fruit cannot. You can tweak the dials in order to gain greater results. You can manipulate the pieces on the game board in order to make the game board more productive for you. There is a way to leverage key items in moments in order to cause the overall bottom line to look much better. All of this in the name of results. If results are the name of the game for you, you will always find a way to apprehend them. There will always be a way to gain access into "greater," "more," "increase," "better," "growth." But at what cost?

John's moment of testing sounded like this, "What are you going to do about it?" If this is the way that it was put to John, maybe yours will sound something like

---

[28] Phil. 1:15-18, NLT

this, "You're no longer being appreciated...what are you going to do about it?" "Your crowds are shrinking and you're losing your influence...what are you going to do about it?" "Everything that you've been working for seems to be falling apart...what are you going to do about it?" "Your platform is being challenged... what are you going to do about it?" "You've got to protect the brand that you've been building...what are you going to do about it?" What are you going to do about it? What will you do about it?

Nothing is worth getting outside of rhythm with God. Not fame. Not fortune. Not the right relationship circle. Not the right selection of opportunities. Nothing. However, know that this will not come for free. It is guaranteed to be tested. It is who you are in the hour of testing and tension that determines whether or not this is something that you "amen" and applaud from a distance, or something that actually gets worked into the fabric of who and what you really are. This is not a truth that can be adopted in language alone; this truth must be lived.

John discerned what had been "given" to him from heaven. Have you identified what has been given to you? Do you know the difference between that and then all the other stuff that has accumulated in your life out of other means? I pray so. And if not, I pray that now the Lord will begin to tug at your heart and bring you back to a beautiful place of synchronization with Him and His will.

FOLLOWABLE AND REPRODUCIBLE

"God has no more precious a gift to a church or an age than a man who lives as an embodiment of his will, and inspires those around him with the faith of what grace can do."[29]

For the next couple of chapters, we will take a look at a man whom God was able to make. This man is known as the apostle Paul. Paul understood that he

---

[29] Andrew Murray, *Grace Quotes*, Men of Integrity, July/August 2000, https://gracequotes.org/quote/god-has-no-more-precious-gift-to-a-church-or-an-ag/.

was a made man. You can hear it in his words; it thunders through. If you remember, it was Paul, in writing to the believers who were gathering in Corinth, who said, "Follow me, as I follow Christ."[30] Another translation says it this way, "Imitate me, just as I also imitate Christ."[31]

These are very strong words. This is not a small claim. Can you imagine someone speaking today and saying such a thing? I mean, the nerve they would have to have. Basically, what Paul is saying here is this, if we could put it into more simple terms, "Follow me. Do everything that I do. Day to day, walk with me, learn from the way that I live. If you do this, I guarantee you that you will not only be able to find a deep, intimate place with the Lord, but God will be able to bring to life every bit of gift and calling in you, and get out of you everything that He desires." All of this is wrapped into Paul's invitation to "follow him," or "imitate him," as he follows Jesus. Wow!

If someone today made such a claim we would be tempted to consider them arrogant. I mean, who would do such a thing? Who would think enough of themselves in order to dare to call a crowd, or a single person, to follow their example? Either someone who is completely full of themselves, or, someone

---

[30] 1 Cor. 11:1, NIV

[31] 1 Cor. 11:1, NKJV

who understands exactly what Paul understood. I do not believe that Paul's claims were out of arrogance at all. I wouldn't believe that or interpret what he is saying that way one bit. In fact, I believe it to be the exact opposite.

Paul was a man that understood what arrogance was all about. Paul was the man who spent a great deal of time imprisoning and beating believers. Paul was the guy that believed he was following God, only to have Jesus encounter him in the middle of his hardest running to reveal that he was working against Him. Sidenote: I love how Jesus is able to step in front of us and knock us off of our high horse when we are arrogantly running, thinking for Him, yet to find out, against Him and things He is working out in the earth. Paul was very aware of what it looked like to be heading in the wrong direction, and leading an entire crowd of people in that same wrong direction. But, continuing in this wrong direction is obviously not how Paul's story ended.

Though Paul was a man familiar with leading people astray, he was also a man who became familiar with an encounter with Jesus. Praise God! Nothing is ever too far gone when you factor in an encounter with Jesus. There is no situation too dark, no circumstance too wrong, when you consider Jesus stepping in front. There is no amount of determination too resilient.

There is no error too great, when you consider Jesus stepping in front.

All things are possible to those who believe, through encounter with God. And Paul was a man that had an encounter with God. Paul's encounter came at the highest point of all that he was seeking to accomplish in the name of God. Then God stepped in and brought Paul to the lowest place. It is from this lowest place that Paul began to understand what it meant to become a made man by God, and not simply a self-made man by his own passions and efforts.

After his encounter, Paul understood that God had really done something in him. This was not a joke. It wasn't some spiritual fabrication for the sake of a perceived benefit. Paul wasn't in any way trying to pretend that Jesus had really done something in him in order to gain influence or advance in some weird way. Paul's life had been wrecked by God, and he knew it.

This is what it is all about. Paul was not only aware of God doing something in him. Paul knew that, like Jesus, he was what God was doing, and what God was looking to use. What do I mean? Can you hear the echoing of Jesus' words in Paul's statement, "Follow me?" It seems that just like Jesus, Paul knew that he was what God desired to use.

God did something in Paul, and now that same God that completely wrecked Paul's idea of who he was and what he was about was now calling people to follow after Paul because of the reality of what He was able to do in Paul. God did something so real in Paul that it made Paul followable. This was not some secret desire of Paul's. I am unwilling to believe that Paul was attempting to capitalize on his encounter with Jesus and what God was doing in his life in order to lay hold of some sort of Kingdom influence.

I do believe that Paul was so impacted by the person of Jesus that it completely transformed him as an individual. I believe that when Paul finally understood who Jesus was and what He was doing that he yielded to, and synergized with, the person of Jesus and became an embodiment of the culture of the Kingdom of God here on the earth. God was not simply calling men to follow a random person. He was calling others to follow a representative of another world and its ways, that person being Paul.

The believers in Corinth are not Paul's only issuing of a statement like this. Let's examine some of Paul's other statements to see if we can highlight some consistency in Paul's belief. "The things you have learned and received and heard and seen in me, practice these things, and the God of peace will be with you."[32]

---

[32] Phil. 4:9

Here is, yet again, another outrageous claim. Do the things that you have learned, received, heard and seen, where? In me, is what Paul says. However, this time the "follow me" claim comes with an incentive, or a promise. The promise of doing whatever you have heard or seen coming out of the life and message of Paul is that God will be with you. Follow all of my example, in walk and talk, and God will be with you in power is what Paul is saying.

Paul's message was not a, "Do as I say and not as I do." Paul said that what they were to observe was in him, his real life, being lived out in God day to day. This is where Paul's source of confidence and power resided, in what God had really done in him to make him something new and powerful. Paul's confidence in being followable was not anchored in some external learned ability or behavior, but in an internal reality of something the Holy Spirit had really forged into the makeup of who he was as a man. Paul didn't just know how to do something; he *was* the something, and this something was being held together by the power of the Spirit working in and with Paul.

Let's take a look at one more statement from Paul to see if we can solidify our claim. "Having so fond an affection for you, we were well-pleased to impart to you not only the gospel of God but also our own lives, because you had become very dear to us."[33] Paul had a very real message, yes. There was also a very real man behind the message. This is the power in what Paul understood, *impart our lives to you*. Paul's confidence was that he walked with the Lord in such a way that was worthy of following; at least God thought so, and that's what matters most. Men can applaud you, but if God won't approve you, you haven't made it.

Would you be able to make such a claim? Do you have the felt confidence that Paul had in order to look at a crowd of people, or even a single person for that matter, and tell them to follow you? Would you want someone following you day to day and observing the way that you live? This is what Paul was inviting them to do. We can't just read past statements like this and not investigate their significance.

> **Men can applaud you, but if God won't approve you, you haven't made it.**

Whether or not you feel you are able to make a statement such as this right now or not, this is where God wants you to be. God wants you to be in a place where you can invite others to follow you. Through encounter with Jesus, let Him make you followable. The world is waiting for someone they can follow and

---

[33] 1 Thess. 2:8

not just listen to. There are many who carry the right information, but have not been through transformational encounter with God to become followable. We must contend for a "Do as I say, and as I do, for herein is the power!"

Regardless of how impressive the game of charades may be that we have perfected, it will never hold up. Keeping people at an arm's length so that they are only able to hear us, and yet never get on the inside to see what we are all about in real time in real life will eventually find us out. No matter how many become impressed with your message, it is always best heard in the context of your real life.

Those who know you best should be able to amen your life, your walk, and your talk.

Those who know you best should be able to amen your life, your walk, and your talk. Don't settle for the place of powerful speech when your real life doesn't teach the same lessons. Paul said, whatever heard or seen, do these things. Whether you hear me speak, or just have a vantage point to watch me live, both should preach to you the reality of God. If there be a great chasm between your talk and your walk, it is time to allow God to close the gap!

MOLDABLE AND EXPORTABLE

Culture: The behaviors and beliefs characteristic of a particular social, ethnic, or age group.

The Kingdom of God has a culture that seeks to overtake men. A cultural influence so great that a man no longer is tossed to and fro by all of the relevant fads and cultural swings that may seek to move him or motivate him. A cultural impression so deep and powerful that a man would be able to live from the inside out, and not the outside in. Absolved from the fleeting changes of attitudes and perspectives, there is a place for man to be free. Completely unhinged from the limitations of cultural acceptance. There is a place of God's influence upon the life of a man where that man becomes a culture unto himself in God.

This man is now the influence. No longer subject to being influenced by the world, this free man has only one dominating influence, that being the presence of the King and the ways of His Kingdom. Our desire in the Lord should be to be brought into such a place as this. Paul knew this desire well. Paul had become a culture unto himself. Paul was now God's influence, and God was using this influence to radically and powerfully change the lives of other men.

This is God's goal in making a man, that that man would no longer be made by his surroundings and the cultural/generational items of the day. Oh, that God would have a man free enough from his surroundings and circumstances to pull others out and into such a wonderful place of freedom! Paul was a man such as this. Paul had been influenced, and was continually being influenced, by the King and the Kingdom, to an extent that was not only any longer just transforming his own life, but now the life of everyone wherever he found himself.

Behaviors from time to time are things that you may know how to do. These behaviors may be performed if situational convenience is leaning in your favor. However, behaviors that have been tested over time and under tension are things that you have now become.

Culture is not just something that happens overnight. The cultural standard of your life is not something that you woke up with today. In fact, you have been developing the culture of your life by either great intentionality, or lack thereof, over time. Your culture was not handed to you; it was allowed by you. No one is going to fight to help you establish the cultural standard you are dreaming of. For most, their culture is only alive in their dreams, and this a nightmare that we should not have to live.

One great way to test the strength of culture in your life that you have been attempting to develop is to introduce another culture to it. We all know how this goes. Have you ever spent time in someone else's home, or had someone, or another family, come to spend time with you in your home? You very quickly realize the truth of the point we are discussing here. It doesn't take long to realize that not everybody is the same as you. People don't share the same life rhythms. They may not share the same values. They may not have the same concerns. They could possibly parent their kids differently. They could interact with their spouse differently. Okay, you get the point.

But what do you do in a situation like we are describing? Do you just bend and yield to the other culture that has been introduced to you? Do you simply forfeit the culture that you have been working so faithfully to establish? This is where some find themselves. In order to create some sense of commonality, they bend. They lose all of their bearings. They call it "adjusting" for the time being. But in the end, everyone loses, especially those that God needed to be influenced by the culture that He has been working to establish in you.

You have probably heard something like this, "You just don't understand what my family is like." Or, how about this one, "The people at my work are just different." Or, this is a really good one too, "They just don't believe the same way that I do, so it's really hard." All of these may seem like great exemptions from being able to uphold the cultural standard that God has developed in you...until you hold them up against the life of someone like the apostle Paul. Paul confronts all of our excuses that we feel hold weight in this conversation.

Paul understood that his lifestyle, or the culture of the Kingdom that his life embodied, was a pattern. It was a pattern that God was using and calling others into it. While writing to the believers in Philippi, Paul said these words, "Brethren, join in following my example, and observe those who walk according to the pattern that you have in us."[34] This pattern that Paul spoke of was the relentless reliance upon the disciplines and attentions that the Holy Spirit had forged in him. Paul knew what the Spirit had done in him, and he wouldn't budge from it.

It didn't matter where Paul found himself, the result was the same. Paul wasn't only effective in one type of setting, or place. This is the point. Paul had been molded by God and now he was being exported by God. Exported? Paul was being shipped out, or sent, to various places around the region to be an influence, to bring the culture of the Kingdom, and more importantly, to bring the presence of the King.

God got what He wanted out of Paul because He had already gotten what He wanted in Paul.

If you listen closely enough you can almost hear it. From God's perspective, you can almost hear these words, "If I can just sow Paul in, and leave him long enough, I am going to get what I want." "If I can just get Paul in, and let him live among them long enough, I know that I will get the outcome that My heart desires."

---

[34] Phil. 3:17

The life of Paul had become God's building program. God was using Paul's life to bring radical transformation wherever Paul went. Ephesus. Thessalonica. Philippi. Corinth. Galatia. Rome. Colossae. It didn't matter where Paul went, God got what He wanted. Can the same be said of you?

God got what He wanted out of Paul because He had already gotten what He wanted in Paul. It was the lifestyle of encounter and the continual influence of the King and His Kingdom on Paul that made him successful. Paul's success wasn't because he was able to own property. Paul didn't have the best worship leader. Paul didn't care what the governmental structure was, or who was in authority where he went. It wasn't because everywhere Paul went the people were favorable to his message. It wasn't because Paul was a fantastic fundraiser. None of these things were it for Paul.

The reality of what God had really done in Paul's life was so authentic, and so powerful, that God chose to use the substance of the life of the man who walked with Him in total surrender. Everything God needed He had put in Paul. It was in him. Wholehearted surrender to the King and His Kingdom is what God is after. God had built a man, and now that man was a wrecking ball.

Is your life one that God knows He can put down anywhere and get the outcome that He is after? Has your life been impacted by the King and the culture of the Kingdom in such a way that you've not only been molded, but now you can be exported? Again, you may not be exported to some distant land, but that is not the point.

Can God send you to your job and get the outcome that He is after? Can God put you down in your family reunion and get the desires that are on His heart accomplished? Are you one that God knows He can sow into a school campus and end up with what He needs to happen? Does God know without a shadow of **Paul's mission was to multiply covenant lovers.** a doubt that you are one who is able to change the cultural dynamic of your household? This is what God is after.

God is building people who can live among others, with a message, yes, but with a life that bears witness to the message. A life that bears witness to the message, the mission, and the reality of substance that God, by the power and processing of the Holy Spirit, has worked into that man or woman. Paul's mission was to multiply covenant lovers. And this is our mission too. The multiplication of covenant lovers, covenant with God and our brother/sister, who will embody the culture of the Kingdom to a degree powerful enough to reproduce Jesus Himself in individuals and communities of love and power.

Are you moldable? Are you exportable? Do you have a confidence in what God has done in you that empowers you to be the influence and not the influenced? If there is any doubt in you about how you need to answer these questions, it is time to begin right now. It is time to start living from the inside out. It is time to begin to see the frailty of the excuses that you may have embraced up until this point in your life as to why your life is not bearing the influence that God desires and allow the Holy Spirit to evict them from your heart by the influence of the King and His Kingdom.

You are the doorway to change that God is waiting to open for people around you.

You are an ambassador. You are a representative. You are one that reveals, or represents the King and the ways of His Kingdom. It is time to not only fight to establish a cultural precedent in your own heart and life, but to allow God to begin using that standard to bring radical and powerful transformation to people and places that He already has placed you. You are the doorway to change that God is waiting to open for people around you. The pattern is being worked into you.

In the next chapter, we will take a look at why it is so important to develop this inside-out type of life. Things that we believe are guarantees on the outside of our life do not remain guarantees forever. If, or when, shaking comes, we need to make sure that we've received something that really will not be shaken.[35] Let us continue on, and take a look at the people of God in Daniel chapter 1.

---

[35] Heb. 12:28, NIV

CHAPTER 07

LUXURIES AND NECESSITIES

"You can see God from anywhere if your mind is set to love and obey Him."[36]

God is really after the making of individuals that would live in intimacy and power. In intimacy and power these individuals transcend their environmental and situational placement with incredible effectiveness to move forward the Kingdom of God. God is into impacting people because He is forming a people. A

---

[36] A. W. Tozer, *The Pursuit of God* (Camp Hill, PA: WingSpread Publishers, 2006), 88.

bride for His Son, without spot, wrinkle, or blemish is God's desire.[37] The forming of one is important, because however great a multitude may be, it is a multitude of ones. God is after the making of the one.

Daniel chapter 1 provides us with an interesting situation that beautifully illustrates our point. Let's turn our attention to the story in the opening verses. "In the third year of the reign of Jehoiakim king of Judah, Nebuchadnezzar king of Babylon came to Jerusalem and besieged it. *The Lord gave Jehoiakim king of Judah into his hand,* along with some of the vessels of the house of God; and he brought them to the land of Shinar, to the house of his god, and he brought the vessels into the treasury of his god."[38]

This is not a favorable situation for God's people. If you are familiar at all with the story, you are aware that things are not going well for them at this point. They are being ripped out of their land. An evil king named Nebuchadnezzar has come in and is conquering them as a people and taking them against their will to be exiles in his kingdom. All of what they were familiar with and had grown accustomed to is being shaken and literally torn away from them in a moment's notice.

---

[37] Eph. 5:27, NLT

[38] Dan. 1:1-2 (emphasis mine)

We gain more details of just how gross of a situation this was a few verses later when we are told that many of them were ordered to now learn the literature and language of the Chaldeans, who were the enemies that they were being forced to now live among.[39] Also, some had to face the challenge of being renamed.[40] Renamed? You can't be serious? Yes, very serious. Meaning, some even had their names changed, and now had to answer to a new name. Talk about a complete shift in perspective of personal identity.

Chaos seems to be abounding in the first couple verses of Daniel chapter 1. God's people have been overwhelmed. Enemies in the land seem to have the upper hand. All of this does not seem to make a lot of sense. This doesn't make sense because this does not seem to be a favorable situation for God's people. How, or why, would God allow all of this to happen? Wouldn't God want His people to be successful? Doesn't He know that this is not going to turn out well?

With all of this happening, there are a couple of words in the second verse of Daniel chapter 1 that just don't seem to fit. The first couple of words of verse 2 say, *"The Lord gave Jehoiakim king of Judah into*

---

[39] Dan. 1:4

[40] Dan. 1:7

his hand..."[41] Wait...what? This cannot be. There is no way that this could be God's will for His people. The God that I know would not willingly hand over any one of His children to an unfavorable situation. The God that I believe in would not dare allow His people to be brought into suffering such as what is being described in Daniel chapter 1. Whose God is this? Because it surely isn't mine, or is it?

All that is thought of in a scenario like this is how troublesome of a situation this truly is. There doesn't seem to be a lot of room for success. Can you imagine? Being torn away from your land. This was a big deal. Being taken captive by a wicked, godless king. No longer being able to worship with your people freely. No longer having the privilege to gather at the temple corporately. Not even being able to study your own history and Scriptures. Everything about the way they did life was immediately turned upside down.

Most would be unwilling to believe that God would allow something like this to happen, but that is because we don't see things from God's perspective. Our view of God, at times, can be very weak. What I mean is this. God is not sitting around in the heavens frantically worrying and falling apart trying to figure out what He is going to do next because of the

---

[41] Dan. 1:2 (emphasis mine)

chaos that seems to be stirring in the earth, or your life specifically for that matter. God is not afraid that some plan of the enemy is going to be too powerful for Him to provide a solution.

Our view of God at times is too fragile. God is unmatched. He has no rival. There is no equal. He is seated. He is at rest. Psalm 2 tells us that He laughs and He scoffs at the rage of the enemy's attempts to dethrone Him and bring disruption to His plans.[42] God has a plan that is always moving forward, a Kingdom that is always expanding, and a people that are always grafted into those promises and purposes.

God has never been afraid of what we call "uncertainty," because everything is always certain with Him.

You need to understand that God is not afraid of hostile situations. God has never been afraid of what we call "uncertainty," because everything is always certain with Him. God is not shaken and afraid when "unfavorable" things happen to you. Why would this be the constant posture that God is enabled to take? God is extremely confident of the powerful work that He is doing in you. God realizes what He has deposited into your life, and the

---

[42] Psalm 2:4

incredible potency of that deposit. What God has put in you, and is doing in you, is far greater than anything that may be happening around you.

The unshakable kingdom that resides on the inside of you does not need the right situational setup in order to be successful. In fact, God has gone to great extremes in order to prove to His people that He was far superior to any of the challenges that they believed would be a limitation to Him being able to be who He says He is in their midst.

God is more confident in His influence upon you than He is the trouble that may surround you in any given moment.

God is confident and secure in Himself. God is overwhelming confident in His influence in and upon you. He is more confident in His influence upon you than He is the trouble that may surround you in any given moment. The real issue is that most times we do not have that same confidence in God, or the work He has done, and is doing, in us.

Not a single one of us would want to be put into a situation like the one that is being described. But of all the reasons that we could provide as to why not, at the heart of the matter one of those reasons would be, because we would be afraid of who and what we would be.

How would we survive? What would we do? Would we make it? Would we compromise? All of these are gripping questions for sure and challenge us to really wrestle honestly with what God has actually done in us and not just what we know how to communicate at times in order to shield our lack of reality. Let's go back to our storyline here from the first couple verses of Daniel.

God's people were in a moment ripped away from everything that defined them as a people. Again, they were torn from their land. They were no longer allowed their religious devotion and expression as a people. This means they couldn't gather publicly for worship, Scripture reading, or anything of the sort. There was no more temple. All of this has had a profound impact on who they believed they were as a people, and more importantly, who they believed God was to them and with them.

Let's make this a little more applicable. Here is how it hits home...You are going to be given a couple of hours to pack a bag. You will board a plane and be dropped off in one of the most violently hostile lands against followers of Jesus. You will be given a new name when you arrive. There aren't any Christian gatherings. No big churches, or small for that matter, with star-studded worship teams and your favorite preachers. Christian Internet content is not allowed in the country you are now living.

You cannot carry a Bible publicly, or have one found in your possession, without being in fear of having your life taken. You don't get to ride around with the windows down blasting worship music on the stereo in your vehicle. You will be forced to learn the language and the history of the new culture that you've been planted into. No more stirring talks of Jesus over your favorite latte in the neighborhood coffee shop. All of the rules of engagement have just radically shifted. This is now your life. This would be the equivalent of what Daniel and all of his people were experiencing.

Who are you going to be in this situation? Do you believe that this could be a setup for success? Is there a way to succeed in a scenario such as this? I believe there is. I believe there is because God believes there is. Again, God has never been intimidated by hostile situations. In fact, God sent His Son from a heavenly "safe" place into a hostile land that got Him killed. God is not afraid to go into dark places with people that don't share the same views and live among them in a way that will offer them freedom and powerfully transform them.

I live in the West, so my experience has been shaped by much of what happens here. What I know to be true about Christianity in the West is this: we enjoy a lot of freedoms. Christianity in the West has the privilege of taking advantage of many, what I would call, luxuries. We will define luxury as something that is nice to have, but may not be necessary. We enjoy a lot of luxuries in the West. I say that because much of our Christian experience and history of engaging with God's people, for the most part, only makes sense here in the West. There are various places in the world right now that have not been awarded the same freedoms and luxuries that are currently being enjoyed by many here in the West.

Actually, to take it a step further, there are places in the world right now that if you tried to start a conversation about the possibility of some of the things that we enjoy freely coming to be a part of their experience there they would laugh because of how unbelievable it would be. Around the world, people are suffering for the Gospel. People are being imprisoned for their declared faith in Jesus. Many are losing their lives for the sake of this faith in Jesus that they are unwilling to recant on. There are very real prices being paid by precious ones that have seen the beauty of the Son of God that they cannot deny.

Much of our experience and history with Christian life in the West doesn't even make sense if attempted in other parts of the world. Much of what we believe is absolutely necessary for our success in walking with God is not even an option in other places. So, if this is the case, how could something that I view as so necessary to me not be an option to another? The question that this must provoke then is this, is what I consider to be a necessity actually a necessity to God? I'm glad you asked. Now we are getting somewhere.

The simple truth that we need to wrestle with in our hearts is that most of what we consider to be necessities are in actuality just luxuries. Most of what you would think you couldn't live a successful life in God without is just a luxury based on preference. God is not concerned with you taking advantage of the luxuries that are made available to you. Not at all.

We will maximize the luxuries while we are at liberty to do so and the use thereof for the glory of God and the furthering of the Kingdom. We will use these luxuries freely to impact as many people as possible for Jesus. However, when these luxuries begin to blind you to the necessities, now we have got a problem. When the luxuries eclipse the necessities, God takes notice. The issue has never been the luxuries in and of themselves. The real issue has always been the placement of these luxuries in the hearts of God's people.

In a moment, the people of God were ripped away from all of what they believed tethered their lives to a place of success in walking with God. Instantly removed from all of what they believed identified them as God's people. The stripping away of identification is not an easy road to travel for some. Some have completely allowed their lives to become absorbed into a type of role, a responsibility, a title that you work from, a position, etc. For some, the removal of this identification in their life is enough to send them spiraling out of control.

Whatever trouble the people of God thought they were in, God had things under control, and He does in your situation too. Again, God is not intimidated one bit by troublesome situations. He shines brightest in the darkest hour. He rises to the occasion greatest against the most impossible challenges. He is the great I AM. And at times we don't realize just how great He is until we are put in a place where it must be proved.

So then, what is necessary to God in order for Him to have His way in you and the people He is forming in your generation? Again, great question. All you need is God. I don't want to oversimplify this at all, but it is true. In the case study that we have been evaluating here God was completely confident with His people just having His presence and each other. God's presence and the presence of His people, that's it? That's it.

Do not become deceived by lights, camera, action, into thinking that God somehow "needs" all of this in order for you to grow in power and intimacy with Him. This is far from the truth. Jesus prayed for us when He said, "The glory which you have given Me I have given to them, that they may be one, just as We are one; I in them and You in Me, that they may be perfected in unity, so that the world will know You sent Me, and loved them, even as You have loved Me."[43]

The work of the Holy Spirit in and among you is more than enough. It's really not difficult in theory. God has made it extremely simple to understand. In fact, I believe that it is so simple that it is offensive, and therefore, men overextend themselves seeking a "new way" or a method that they can claim credit for.

Don't allow your heart and life to become cluttered by luxuries that will rob you of the power of the necessities.

This is God's prescription: worship, prayer, fasting, the Scriptures, fellowship, and shared meals. At least this is what we find in the book of Acts chapter 2.[44] The programming is simple, yet powerful when applied. It may not be greatly applauded because of the flash and the flare that it lacks, but it sure does shine to God. And His people shine best when His

---

[43] John 17:22-23
[44] Acts 2:42-46

prescription is applied, no matter where they are or what they may seem to be facing.

Allow God to sift through your heart to find out how much of your walk and current experience is based off of luxuries and preferences. Don't allow your heart and life to become cluttered by luxuries that will rob you of the power of the necessities. God's deposit and work in you is incredibly powerful. Sometimes you have to have the luxuries stripped or shaken in order to find out what you are really made of…or better put, what God is really made of in you!

INDIVIDUALITY AND LEGACY

"Not by might nor by power, but by My Spirit," says the Lord of hosts.[45]

Man has a terrible tendency to put himself in the center of everything that God seems to be doing. It is the innate nature in a man that attempts to allow himself to be the center of God's doings. In our contemporary language, we would consider this to be self-centered. Self-centered in the sense of man

---

[45] Zech. 4:6

thinking that he is the primary beneficiary of anything and everything that God seems to be doing that directly involves him.

It is the thought that says somehow, someway that man must be able to increase or gain an advantage by the work of God that is happening to him, or with him, in any given moment. We are not talking about you right now because I know that you are not like this; this is not something that is a struggle for you.

Man has a persuasion in his heart to think that all of what God is doing in him and around him is directly pointing to him. The powerful points of vision that have been deposited into that man must have come with the great intention to be a blessing to that man, otherwise why would God be doing what He seems to be doing at all? In this line of thinking there is a value that is generated by the happenings of a man's involvement with the vision or the encounter that is brought into the life of that man. This type of thinking is very limited in its fullest operation because it causes the story of God to be too small and to end abruptly, or too short.

The culture of our current day has become very individualistic. Everything points to the individual. Truth is relative to a person's feelings, therefore dismantling any chance of believed absolute truths. Happiness is directly connected to the individual pursuit of an individual and what would cause them to be happy, as they see or define happy. Nothing seems to matter anymore except how any individual decides they will choose to interpret and then engage whatever situation they may be in. Whatever they may feel is appropriate for them, this is to then be accepted and celebrated by all.

It is no wonder this type of thinking has infiltrated the lives of followers of Jesus. This type of thinking

God's heart is not only positioned for what is happening in any given moment, but also how that one moment is affecting moments that are yet to happen.

has permeated His body like a cancer. God desires to bring a great purging to His body to rid it of this individualistic thinking. Being individualistic is not the same as celebrating individuality. Individuality says that you are unique. Individualistic says that you are independent.

This individualistic thinking has damaging repercussions because it causes a man to only think of himself, the moment that he is living in, and the benefit being created for himself. God's heart is not only positioned for what is happening in any given moment, but also how that one moment is affecting moments that are yet to happen. Our God is a God of generations, generational impact, and generational momentum. God is in the past, the present, and the future, all at once, right now, without limitation to time as our minds and lives experience it and understand it.

God has chosen to reveal himself in this way: The God of Abraham, the God of Isaac, and the God of Jacob.[46] This was a revelation that God gave to Moses as He was speaking to him from the burning bush. This is an incredible moment in Moses' life. Moses is wrapped up in a life-changing encounter with God. This is an experience that would alter the trajectory and speed of Moses' life in a very profound way.

Moses would go from the back side of a wilderness tending to sheep, to now being thrusted into a national position of prominence and power fully equipped with signs, wonders, and miracles to assist in all of what God had spoken to him. This encounter with God completely transformed the man, Moses, and ushered him into a new season with God.

However, in line with our point that we are building I would like to shed light on some wonderful things about Moses' encounter that oftentimes is easy to breeze by and overlook completely. Moses has a profound encounter with God that directly affected his life and the calling of his life, yes. But, regardless of how good this might seem for Moses, let's take a

---

[46] Ex. 3:6

close look at the "why" this seems to happen to Moses. God does not come to Moses simply for the sake of Moses. God's reasoning is actually quite different. We will pick up the story in verse 7 of Exodus chapter 3:

And the Lord said: "I have surely seen the oppression of My people who are in Egypt, and have heard their cry because of their task-masters, for I know their sorrows. So, I have come down to deliver them out of the hand of the Egyptians, and to bring them up from that land to a good and large land, to a land flowing with milk and honey, to the place of the Canaanites and the Hittites and the Amorites and the Perizzites and the Hivites and the Jebusites. Now therefore, behold, the cry of the children of Israel has come to Me, and I have also seen the oppression with which the Egyptians oppress them. Come now, there-fore, and I will send you to Pharaoh that you may bring My people, the children of Israel, out of Egypt."[47]

Wow! Did you read that the same way that I did? Maybe you didn't, and I don't want you to miss it so I'll

---

[47] Ex. 3:7-10, NKJV

explain what it is that I see here when reading over these verses. Moses is standing in front of the burning bush in a holy moment with God. God tells Moses, "Moses, things are about to change dramatically for you. Moses, I am about to turn the table on things happening to you and the children of Israel. In fact, Moses, I am going to raise you up and use you in a mighty way. You are about to be a man of incredible influence. You are about to be a man of great declaration and demonstration. I am going to use you to deliver an entire nation, My people, from the captivity of Pharaoh and the bondage to slavery they are experiencing. Moses, I am about to use your life in an amazing way to change history!"

God is a master at walking men into outcomes that don't line up with their résumés.

All of this sounds incredible. It sounds overwhelming to consider the way that God comes to men and speaks of endings that don't seem to match their beginnings. God is a master at walking men into outcomes that don't line up with their résumés. This is where Moses was standing. After his upbringing in luxury to then being in the wilderness, God comes with the burning bush encounter and propels him into a whirlwind that would shake Pharaoh's entire kingdom. This is the God that we walk with! God is able to turn things in a moment for Moses.

However incredible this sounds, it is very important that we take note that these are not the only details. God tells Moses, "I have surely seen the oppression of My people who are in Egypt, and have heard their cry because of their taskmasters, for I know their sorrows. So, I have come down to deliver them…"[48] Essentially what God is saying to Moses is this, "I am going to use you…but it is not only because of you."

It wasn't just because Moses had the goods. It wasn't just because of Moses' intellect, his relational network strength, his ability or gifting. I am sure that Moses was a capable guy, but this is not the primary reason that God came looking for him. And in most cases, it is not the reason that God comes looking for you either.

God had a vision that was bigger than Moses. God had a plan that didn't only affect the life of Moses. It should be alarming to you when you see a man or a woman stand up who claims to have a vision from God that doesn't affect anyone other than them. If they are the only one that seems to benefit; if they are the only one that seems to get exalted; if they are the only one that gains influence; if they are the only one

---

[48] Ex. 3:7-8, NKJV

that benefits financially; if they are the only one that seems to get pushed into the light…it is a problem. It is a problem because any real vision from God doesn't just affect one person.

God is not self-centered. God is a space maker. God is looking to make room for others. God is secure enough in Himself to make space for others. God came looking for a man that he could not only look to, but through. Here is the key issue.

It is not that God had a total disregard for Moses. It is just that God is looking for a man that would be willing to lay himself down in order to see others lifted up. It is an unavoidable thought process for God because

God is secure enough in Himself to make space for others.

that is who God is; one who lays down His life in order to lift others. God lays His life down to make space for others. God was looking at Moses, and through Moses at the same time, at the children of Israel, His covenant people, whose cries He was hearing.

There was a covenant people that God wanted to be faithful to, and raising up Moses was the way that he was choosing to do it. Moses' greatness became a demonstration of God's faithfulness to His people. And I believe that it is with that same intention today that God raises men.

Do you have a vision that is bigger than you? Do you have a vision that includes anyone other than you? If you don't, you may have a good vision, but you don't yet have a God vision. God is looking to use your life to make space for others. God was looking to provide an answer to the children of Israel and what they were going through...Moses became that answer. Are you ready to allow God to make your life an answer?

There is a covenant cry that is raising from the earth that God desperately wants to respond to. He is looking for a person through whom He can do that. Are you that person? Would you allow God, in the place of encounter, to make your life an answer to the cry of this generation?

God may lift you, but not solely just because of you. God is looking for you to lift others, make space for others, use what He is doing in you to bring others along. We have to stop viewing our own personal encounter as something that has come to us just solely to be a blessing or benefit to us. This is not the case. We must begin to see encounter through the lens of legacy and not just individuality. Encounter, if we would realize it, has more to do with legacy than it does individuality.

You have to stop thinking about your encounter with God as something that only impacts you. Your encounter with God is not just something that is for you. Your encounter, as it was with Moses, is not just something that is looking at only you. Your encounter is looking at you, yes, but also simultaneously looking through you to all of the lives that will be affected by you. God uses your encounter for you and for countless others through you. The possibilities of all of the lives that will be impacted by your personal encounter with God are endless.

You must allow the Holy Spirit to shift your thinking from an individualistic mentality. There are many others that are greatly affected by whatever may seem like a personal, individual experience that you may have with God. Why is this? How could this be? Why would it matter? These are all great questions, and valid thoughts to have.

Simply put, other people suffer when you are not who God needs you to be. You are not the only person who "feels it" when you are not walking with God in the place of encounter and obedience. There are others around you in your various spheres of influence and responsibility that also "feel it" when you are not correctly in alignment with God.

When you are not walking with God as you should be it has a ripple effect. The ripple effect that we are describing here is one that is extremely difficult to quantify. However, know this. It far extends beyond what you or I are able to fathom. This is one of the reasons it is so important that we pay attention to encounter, and the byproducts of encounter that God has in mind, as it was in the life of Moses.

When you are experiencing God in a personal, private way, it has the potential to have a public effect. The outcome of you experiencing God in private, or personally, is that other people's lives are impacted and greatly influenced. God is able to use the life of the man that He is personally influencing to make his life a public influence.

Personal turns to public when you are encountering God and walking faithfully with Him.

Personal turns to public when you are encountering God and walking faithfully with Him. There is no way around this; it is a perfectly drawn conclusion by God Himself. Your definition of public means whoever else is involved in your life that is beyond you. Public means anyone more than you. Your spouse, your children, your coworkers, your employees, your classmates, your teammates, etc., and the list goes on and on and on.

The possibilities of public impact are profound. Your impact on one other person's life is not left with that one person alone. You impact a coworker who then goes on to impact his entire sphere of influence. Their family can be influenced. Their spouse is impacted. Their children get impacted. It doesn't just stay here. All of the people that they now interact with are going to be influenced, and all because of what is happening, or has happened, in person A's life.

A person that is in any of their spheres of influence may have a profile or responsibility that then powerfully impacts an entire nation! Nations are now being changed because of what has been pointed all the way back to an encounter that happened with one person. When you sit down and attempt to draw out all of the connecting pieces that are opened up because of one encounter it becomes mind boggling to think of all that God is able to do because of the way that He encounters one person.

Isaiah tells us that God thinks very differently from us. Also, that God's ways are not like our ways.[49] God's ways are very different from human reasoning, He is other than, He is holy, set apart. God is not thinking in individualistic terms. God is not thinking selfishly with what He is doing and how He is accomplishing His plans. In other words, He is not only thinking about himself.

We must allow transformation to come to our lives by the renewing of our minds, so that we can gain this powerful perspective.[50] It takes a real work of the

---

[49] Isa. 55:8
[50] Rom. 12:2

Spirit in our hearts and minds to be free to think of benefitting others without some sort of self-benefit involved in the equation.

Your life is to be lived out for the sake of legacy and not just personal gain in the place of individuality. Legacy, by definition, is something that is handed down, or gifted, by a predecessor. A predecessor is someone that has gone before you. A predecessor can also be thought of as someone that has made it somewhere, or into something, that you haven't; they have gone before you. Using these definitions, legacy then means that God is using you to break into things in the place of encounter that will be passed on to others around you.

Legacy means that God is using you to break into things in the place of encounter that will be passed on to others around you.

The children of Israel experienced deliverance from captivity and the oppression of hundreds of years by a wicked, godless pharaoh because Moses had an encounter with God and then faithfully walked out the implications of that encounter with God. This is overwhelming to consider. Your "yes" to God in encounter today is influencing people tomorrow, and possibly hundreds of years from now.

God was looking into Moses' yes and what that would mean for the Egyptians, Pharaoh, the children of Israel in the moment, and all of those that would forever be impacted because of that encounter. People are still being impacted today and lives are being changed because of Moses' encounter with God in the burning bush.

Do not minimize the importance or the effect of personal encounter and the potential it contains. There is a powerful legacy that is still flowing that I am sure Moses didn't have a grid to understand the significance thereof in the moment.

The apostle Paul is another great example. Because of Paul's encounter with God in the book of Acts chapter 9, countless lives have been impacted.[51] But this is God's way. Again, this is unavoidable. What God is doing in your life is being passed on to those around you. Countless others are being impacted by who God is making you.

When God was looking at Paul, He was also looking at Galatia, Ephesus, Corinth, Philippi, Thessalonica, Rome...and you and me! This is incredible! You and I were thought of when God encountered Paul. God, looking through Paul, was looking to you and me. Thousands of years after Paul, we

---

[51] Acts 9:3-9

are still being impacted by the ripple effect of Paul's encounter with God.

The reverse of this is equally true, and it must be this way in order for balance to be found in the equation. When you are not living faithfully with God in the place of encounter, others suffer the consequence along with you. When you are not walking the way you should, God has to look for someone else to use to bring impact to the lives of those who are not able to receive that impact from your life. This should be a very sobering thought.

Your spouse suffers when you are not yielded to God in the place of encounter. Your children suffer when you are not encountering God and living it out faithfully. Your friends and those close to you suffer when you are not encountering God and living it out faithfully. The sphere gets bigger and bigger and the implications go further and further.

And whether negative or positive, this doesn't have an age limit attached to it. If you are a young person, or young adult, going to school and possibly working a job, you are not exempt from the discussion. Your friends need you. Your classmates need you. Your coworkers need you. They need you to be who God is making you in the place of encounter. All of these people need the influence that reverberates off of your life when you are encountering God in a personal, private way, and then allowing God to speak to others and powerfully touch others through your life of walking with Him in faithful obedience.

This truth is not waiting for you to become a specific age so that it is relevant, or so that it will then apply at a future date. If you are walking with God, regardless of your age, this is speaking directly to you... and pointing through you to others.

Others will be who they are because you allowed God to do in you what He needed to do.

When we live with ourselves in the center of the story as the catchall and end-all, the story becomes too small and ends too short. God doesn't have the opportunity to extend His-Story through our lives when we limit the details to ourselves. When we allow God to extend His-Story through us and point to others, He will continue to make history with and through us. Sometimes you will have the blessing of knowing that your life is influencing others or having a profound impact on others in your sphere.

However, the greatest blessing will be received when we all gather around the throne of God together and you are able to have God inform you of all of the people that He was able to powerfully transform because of a seed that was sown into your life through encounter. Others will be who they are because you allowed God to do in you what He needed to do. Your yes to God will make space for others and give them the opportunity to say yes to God in whatever capacity it is that He is coming to them.

Allow God to expand and extend your story by taking your eyes off of you. Pray for the Holy Spirit to begin to break your perspective wide open to the others that are being impacted and influenced by what God is doing in you. Pray that God would give you a confidence to live your life for more than just the moment and to help you to understand that there is a legacy being built through you.

Your life is passing on something to others. The question is, is it something that you are proud to pass? Is it something that is causing others to come alive in God and be better positioned to fulfill their destiny? Or is what is being passed on something that is being used as a lesson in what not to do and how not to live? The choice is yours.

SPEAKING AND YIELDING

"Obedience is not measured by our ability to obey laws and principles; obedience is measured by our ability to obey God's voice."[52]

This segment is one that is near and dear to my heart. It is near and dear to my heart because I have made a personal commitment before God to empty my life into obedience to whatever it is that I feel He is saying to me. This may sound extremely invigorating.

---

[52] Bill Johnson, *AZ Quotes,* http://www.azquotes.com/author/18329-Bill_Johnson?p=2.

Statements like this may be applauded. But to all of those who have a real, deep, intimate connection with the Lord, you know the weight of a statement such as this, and the cost that should be counted by allowing these words to pass over the threshold of your lips.

A commitment to obeying the Lord sounds amazing, so long as God is saying things to you that you find great excitement in obeying. God speaking to you may be perceived as delightful so long as you are able to generate a sense of excitement directly connected into what you know God is saying in the moment. This allows for the use of excitement as empowerment for being able to obey. This is when it could be viewed as much easier to obey the Lord, when there doesn't seem to be any great pain or loss in obeying.

But what about when God begins to talk about things that you do not want to hear? What about when God begins to dig into subjects or situations that are not that easily embraced? Has God ever said something to you in the place of encounter that you didn't want to hear? Has God ever come knocking on your door and issued a statement that you really didn't want to give your attention to? Has there ever been a time where you heard something from God that you just flat out did not want to do?

I would hate to paint the picture to seem as if everyone that has ever heard from God has come away with this fairy tale picture-perfect ending. What about the struggle? What about those who are challenged to obey the Lord? What about those who just simply don't agree with God's perspective or selection? What about those who end up wrestling with God for a time over what they know God wants them to do? There must be a place for an individual such as this, right? Absolutely, and once again, I am so glad that you asked.

Over the years that I have walked with God I have come to learn a simple truth that has had an incredibly profound impact on shaping my life. I guess you could say that it is simply profound, and it is this: Who you really are is whatever the distance is between God's speaking and your yielding. We can sum it up that simply. This is one of the great ways that we can find out where we are with God. You are whatever space can be found between what the place of you recognizing what God is saying to you, and whatever point you in turn obey that word. The distance between those two points is who you are. This is one of the great tools that we can use to determine where we really are in our walk with God.

> **Who you really are is whatever the distance is between God's speaking and your yielding.**

If there is a chance that you do not like the conclusion that you just came to as you considered what an answer to the question may look like, I am sorry. That distance is there because there is something that you have not been doing, that you should start doing a lot quicker than what has created this history. This is not a conclusion that you can throw a fancy coat of paint on and all of a sudden give the appearance as if it became brand new. In fact, this is not even something that can be seen from the outside of your life, and herein is where we find the greatest challenge with this point; it is only visible to you and God.

Have you read the story of Jonah in the Bible? If not, I encourage you to do so. It is one that is filled with great encouragement and wonder. We will discuss in part some of Jonah's story because it provides great insight into the matters we are discussing now.

Jonah is a man that had a walk with God. Jonah had a walk with God and, from what there is recorded about his life, heard clearly from God at times. Jonah heard clearly from God, however, didn't always hear things that he was excited about. In fact, not only did Jonah not hear things that he was excited about, there were times when Jonah heard things that he just flat out chose that he didn't like, and that he would not obey. We will pick up Jonah's story in the first couple of verses of chapter 1.

The word of the Lord came to Jonah the son of Amattai saying, "Arise, go to Nineveh the great city and cry out against it, for their wickedness has come up before Me." But Jonah rose up to flee to Tarshish from the presence of the Lord. So, he went down to Joppa..."[53] Jonah has a moment where he hears clearly what it is that God is saying to him: "Go to Nineveh and preach against the wickedness of that city."

Doesn't seem complicated. Doesn't seem as if there is a lot of wiggle room here for misinterpretation. God has made it very simple. However simple it may seem, Jonah is not finding the willingness from within himself to align himself in obedience to what he knows God is saying to him.

Jonah chooses that he doesn't really like what God is saying and, according to the details given to us in the account, he flees from the presence of the Lord.[54] Jonah has encountered a God that he really doesn't understand. He doesn't want to go to Nineveh and preach to the people there. Jonah can't seem to figure out why God would want to open the door to repentance to such a wicked people. Jonah's opinion of Nineveh was that they didn't deserve the message that God wanted to deliver to them.

---

[53] Jonah 1:1-3

[54] Jonah 1:3

Have you ever encountered God and found out that at times you don't really understand Him? Have you ever encountered God and come to the conclusion that He is other than you would want Him to be? Have you realized yet that God truly is "other than?" He is set apart. At times, this God that is set apart is going to do things that confound the wisdom by which this natural world operates.

But, haven't we already established this point? His ways are not our ways, and His thoughts are not our thoughts.[55] Because of what God revealed to Jonah, Jonah is running from God. Jonah is running from a God that he doesn't really understand and doesn't at all agree with in this point.

Now things get really interesting for Jonah. Without taking too much time we will summarize a longer story. Jonah ends up in a ton of trouble. Life completely turns upside down for him, and those around him, because he is not obeying the word of the Lord for his life. Jonah ends up at the bottom of the ocean in the mouth of a whale for three days. At this point, Jonah determines he is going to lift his head back to God and give God his full attention.

God rescues Jonah. When God rescues Jonah, the Bible says that the word of the Lord came to Jonah a

---

[55] Isa. 55:8

second time. The word that comes to Jonah the second time is the exact same word that came to Jonah the first time that he determined he didn't want to obey, which then sent him running from the presence of the Lord. Jonah finally decides to go to Nineveh to preach against that wicked city. We will resume the story in chapter 3.

Then Jonah began to go through the city one day's walk; and he cried out and said, "Yet forty days and Nineveh will be overthrown." Then the people of Nineveh believed in God; and they called a fast and put on sackcloth from the greatest to the least of them."[56] This is amazing! Jonah went and did what God was asking of him to do and all of the people of Nineveh turned from their sin and chose to believe God and called a fast! This is wonderful! The Bible even says in the last verse of chapter 3 that when God saw their deeds, they turned from their wicked way, then God relented concerning the calamity which He had declared He would bring upon them. And He did not do it.[57]

Surely by seeing the effectiveness of his obedience to the Lord Jonah would've been able to have a change of heart; you would think so. But, he didn't. Jonah was still not happy with God. And this is where

[56] Jonah 3:4-5
[57] Jonah 3:10

we will find our final, and very important point about Jonah's life.

But it greatly displeased Jonah and he became angry. He prayed to the Lord and said, "Please Lord, was not this what I said while I was still in my own country? Therefore, in order to forestall this, I fled to Tarshish, for I knew that you are a gracious and compassionate God, slow to anger and abundant in lovingkindness, and one who relents concerning calamity. Therefore, now, O Lord, please take my life from me, for death is better to me than life. The Lord said, "Do you have good reason to be angry?"[58]

This isn't making a whole bunch of sense. Let's retrace some of the details that brought us to this point. Jonah hears from God. Jonah doesn't want to do what God says, so he turns and flees from His presence. Jonah gets into a lot of trouble. Jonah turns his attention back to God. God rescues Jonah. God speaks to Jonah again, which happens to be the same thing He spoke to him in the beginning.

Jonah obeys this time. Jonah goes to Nineveh and preaches. All of Nineveh turns to God and calls a fast. God turns from the destruction that He intended to bring on Nineveh and all of the people are spared.

[58] Jonah 4:1-4

And now Jonah is angry with God and wants to die. Huh? Somehow, I didn't see that one coming.

Jonah paints the picture for us of a man who on the outside deserves to be greatly celebrated; however, on the inside desperately needs to be calibrated. Jonah gives us a glimpse into the life of a man that doesn't have it all together, yet because of God's amazing love and desire to be in real relationship with His creation, chooses to use in spite of the lack of real change in Jonah because of it. What is incredible to think about, and actually very sobering to think about is this... God uses Jonah. All of Nineveh changes, yet Jonah doesn't change. God can change an entire wicked city through the life of Jonah, but can't change Jonah.

The world celebrates for what is visible on the outside, and God's heart breaks for what needs to be calibrated greatly on the inside.

The world watches and celebrates your movement with God. However, what the world most times doesn't have any clue about is that it took God a great amount of time and effort to actually move you. The world celebrates for what is visible on the outside, and God's heart breaks for what needs to be calibrated greatly on the inside.

The people are cheering, the crowds are applauding, when all the while they have no idea that you didn't even want to be there. Not only did you not want to be there, but you are angry with God because of all of it. This point about Jonah's life teaches us that we must be very careful not to allow the lavishing of celebration on the outside when you know very well just how bankrupt, or misaligned, you can be at times on the inside.

This is crazy to think about. This is also a very dangerous place that we are talking about. It is dangerous if you allow your life to fall into this gap. People celebrating you on the outside; God desperately trying to deal with you on the inside. Again, the real you can be found in whatever the distance is between God's speaking and your yielding.

This just simply can't be faked. I don't believe that Jonah was fake. I believe that he could really see God. I believe he could see the people that God wanted to change. I just also believe that he excluded himself from the conversation of those people that really needed to be changed.

Don't exclude yourself from the conversation. Allow your heart to remain sensitive to God and His speaking. Allow your heart to remain sensitive to hear from God, not just about things for you to go and do, but also, and most importantly, things that He is trying to do and change in you.

AFTERWORD

God's chief goal for man is to fill him with Himself. For God knows that man's only hope of being internally detached from the lustful passions of their world that holds them captive is to be filled with the One that is free from it, Himself. Man's only hope and remedy to his rebellion and inherent desire for independence from God is to be filled with and by God Himself. God desires for man to experience a life of internal freedom from the captivity and oppressors of this life. That freedom is only found by man engaging God's prescribed door to this freedom, Jesus the Son.

- Jesus frees men from rebellion, for He is surrendered to the Father.
- Jesus frees men from independence, for He has eternally laid His life down.
- Jesus is not a captor; He's a savior, saving men from a life of being absorbed into the prison of themselves.

Men desire to do great things, but God desires to make great men. The heart so easily becomes entangled with satisfaction that is sourced by things other than God Himself. The desire for greatness is one that must continually be crucified lest it become the spiritual fuel of exploits that lead men away from God Himself while running with godly activities. The pursuit of passions, power, and prestige will never effectively substitute the life of God that comes from His presence. God's presence is His person, and His Person is His presence.

God can change the world *with* broken men. However, God wants to change the world *of* broken men. There is not enough emphasis in our day on real transformation that comes from being influenced by the presence and person of God Himself. We have people who can prophesy and read your mail, they can supposedly tell you what God is saying, yet have no idea what God has said for they are not familiar with the person of God already revealed in their Bibles. There are those who can lay their hands on the sick and see wonderful, incredible miracles, yet carry a cancer in their own heart of being disconnected from God Himself in a real, deep, intimate way.

It is amazing to me the lengths that people will go to not spend time with God. For so much in our world seems to be easier than going into your closet and closing the door.[59] People would rather spend hundreds of dollars to get in front of someone rather than taking the time to get in front of God. Chasing down a "word" from God at the popular conference. Making sure to stand in the right prayer line so that you can get someone's hand laid on you. Seeking out that prophetic person in your life that you know clearly hears from God in order to obtain a word from God about where you are and what is going on around you.

I have never seen Him and thought about asking for anything other than Him.

All of these may have their place, in a specific time and purpose from the Lord. However, none of these will be substitutes for you spending time with God for yourself and being influenced by Him in a personal way. The strength of your spiritual life is completely dependent on if you actually know Him, and the depth of that knowing. The depth of that knowing is what is forging the real substance in your life. Substance cannot be substituted.

I have never seen Him and thought about asking for anything other than Him. Once you see Him, there is nothing else worth asking for. Once you have

---

[59] Matt. 6:6

caught a glimpse of Him, nothing else in all of the world seems to be able to stand next to His beauty.

I am believing that as you close this book and go into whatever life may have for you that you would be overtaken by a clear vision of Jesus. I am praying that God, by the Holy Spirit, would brand your eyes with a vision of His Son, Jesus. That the entirety of your life from this point forward would be given over to a raw, real, vulnerable pursuit of deep, intimate knowing of Jesus and His ways. I pray that God's desire would become a reality in your life!

ABOUT THE AUTHOR

Michael is the Founding Director of Burning Ones. At the age of twenty-one Michael was a drug addict, dealer, diseased, and hopeless. It was at this time that he had an encounter with Jesus that radically changed his life. From this point forward he has been relentless in his pursuit of the God-Man, Jesus Christ. Michael now preaches Jesus around the world powerfully with great demonstrations of signs and miracles.

You can find out more about Burning Ones
by visiting:

www.burningones.org
www.facebook.com/burningonesinternational

More about Michael:

www.facebook.com/michaelsdow
www.twitter.com/michaeldow
www.instagram.com/michaeldow

ABOUT THE MINISTRY

Burning Ones is the ministry of Michael and Anna Dow. Our vision is to raise up burning ones that will make Jesus famous among the nations of the world. We do that by preaching the Gospel of the Kingdom until the hearts of men and women come alive to God and burn with passion for His Son, Jesus, by the power of the Holy Spirit. We preach Jesus in church services, conferences, and mass crusades around the world with extraordinary signs and miracles.

When He consumes our lives, we become His burning ones! We are burning ones by experience and expression. We experience Him and then we express Him to the world. Burning Ones is not something that is exclusive for us to a specific time and space; it is life itself!

Website: www.burningones.org
Facebook: burningonesinternational
E-mail: info@burningones.org

FREE INDEED

Does God have to have your agreement in order for Him to have your obedience? Will you obey the call of God even if there is not an instant payout or benefit to you? Many are willing to step into obedience and do what God is asking so long as they are the primary beneficiaries of their obedience. Are you willing to walk with a God that you cannot control? Can you handle walking with a Jesus that you cannot manipulate and leverage your faithfulness against? There is a confrontation that awaits you in the text...a confrontation to determine what kind of Jesus follower you are going to be. In the book *Free Indeed*, Michael challenges the reader to surrender everything to Jesus and invest the rest of their life into uncompromised obedience to Him.

Available at:

Amazon
Kindle
iBooks
www.burningones.org

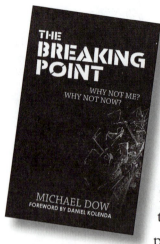

THE BREAKING POINT

Every generation God seeks after a man or a woman that He can use to partner with Him in changing the world. Our lives are the point through which God is desperately longing to break into a generation! What would it look like if God were to truly break into the heart of a man? How would that man impact a generation? Michael challenges the reader to believe that they are the breaking point, right here, right now!

Available at:

Amazon

Kindle

iBooks

www.burningones.org

FASTING

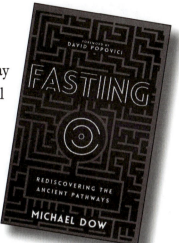

There is an ancient pathway that leads to an endless well of great experience. It is Jesus Christ, alive from the dead, beckoning hearts that burn for Him, "Walk this way…come and find Me here!" In his book, *Fasting*, Michael challenges us to find a greater place of experiential union with Jesus by adventuring out into the deep waters of fasting as a lifestyle.

"Fasting revives the gaze that has lost its fascination with Christ."

"Only the truly hungry will fast."

"Fasting is much more than simply turning from food. Fasting is intentionally and intimately turning to Jesus."

Available at:

Amazon
Kindle
iBooks
www.burningones.org